Beautiful You!

The All About You Guide to Looking and Feeling Your Best

Beautiful You!

The All About You Guide to Looking and Feeling Your Best

By Lori Moore Stacy

SCHOLASTIC INC.
New York Toronto London Auckland Sydney
Mexico City New Delhi Hong Kong

Front cover photos, clockwise from top: Photographer/Jon McKee; Photographer/Jon McKee & Manicurist/Nadine T. Galli; Photographer/Nick Horne

Back cover photo: Photographer/Jon McKee

ISBN 0-439-15531-2

12 11 10 9 8 7 6 5 4 3   0 1 2 3 4 5/0

Printed in the U.S.A.   01

First Scholastic Trade paperback printing, February 2000

Special thanks to:
Roxanne Camron and Sara Fiedelholtz of Petersen's Youth Group; Allison Black, MD, for her expertise on skin care and dermatology; Ronald Lee, DDS, for his expertise on dental care; and Katherine Moore for her expert opinions on being a girl!

Contents

Introduction
All About This Book

How would you describe yourself to a friend you haven't met yet? No doubt you'd tell her about yourself, your friends, your likes and dislikes, where you live . . . and also about the way you look. Your physical appearance is a part of who you are. And while it's nowhere near as important as the inner you — things like your warmth, talent, creativity, personality, good deeds, and intelligence — feeling good about your appearance is important.

This book is designed to give you the basics on caring for your looks from head to toe, as well as from within. You'll learn how to keep your skin, smile, nails, and hair looking their best. You'll find out how to put a wardrobe together that's right for you — and that won't cost a fortune! You'll also find out how important a proper diet and physical activity are to your looks. In sum, this book will give you a healthy perspective on yourself, as well as good grooming habits that we hope will last a lifetime!

Chapter One
Beauty Basics

The Skinny on your Skin

Your skin is your body's largest organ — it's there to shield you from injury; protect you from dirt, germs, and bacteria; and regulate your body temperature. It's constantly renewing itself, with new skin replacing dead outer layers that are shed daily. And when it's injured, your skin has an efficient repair system to patch things up.

Since your skin takes such good care of you, shouldn't you do the same for it? This section is about caring for your skin. You'll learn how to keep it clean and how to protect it. You'll also meet some of your skin's biggest enemies — things like the sun and the weather.

1

Your skin has very unique needs. These needs will change as the weather changes and as you get older. It's important to establish good grooming habits now. They'll keep your skin looking great today and in the future.

Coming clean

Between the natural oils your skin produces and the dirt it picks up throughout the day, you can see why it's important to clean your skin every day. A warm bath or shower a day will get rid of dirt and odor. Use a bar soap or body wash, and don't forget those easy-to-overlook places, like your feet, back, and ears.

A washcloth or bath sponge can help you reach hard-to-get spots, but beware: Bacteria can grow in damp washcloths and sponges. Use a clean washcloth each time you bathe, and be sure to keep bath sponges in a well-ventilated place so they can dry completely. Nylon mesh sponges are another good alternative and aren't as likely to breed bacteria.

Because your face is exposed to air, to food, and to your touch, you should wash it twice a day, once in the morning and once before bed. Choose a facial cleansing bar or nonabrasive cleanser. Deodorant soaps — the ones you use to rub-a-dub-dub in the tub or shower —

may be too harsh for your delicate face. And besides, your face doesn't really need to be deodorized! Try a few different products until you find the one that leaves your face feeling clean but not tight. If you develop redness or a rash, stop using the product immediately. You could be allergic to one of the ingredients.

Use warm water to wash your face — hot water is too drying and cold water won't penetrate the pores as well (nor will it be very comfortable). While splashing water a few times on your face usually gets the grime off, you can also opt to use a soft washcloth. Gently rub your face with the washcloth to help remove dead top layers from your skin. Be careful not to scrub, though — that could irritate your skin. Abrasive cleansers or pads are another definite no. They'll irritate and dry out your skin as well. Also be sure to get all the soap or cleanser off your skin — the residue can cause dryness.

Don't go overboard on skin-care products. Unless your skin is completely damaged (such as when it's sunburned), you really don't need much more besides good ole soap and water. Your skin is pretty efficient at your age — it produces oil when it needs it and replaces dead skin with fresh new skin. Toners, astringents, face moisturizers, eye creams, and the hundreds of other products that are out there aren't nearly as efficient at keeping your skin in good condition as your skin itself!

The pimple problem

A pimple, or acne, is formed when the pores in your skin are blocked with excess oil or dirt and become inflamed. As you jump headfirst into puberty, your hormones will become more active. These hormones trigger a bunch of things, including everything that's happening under the surface of your skin. Stress can get your hormones churning, too. You can also thank your parents when pimples show up: Acne is hereditary — teens whose parents had skin problems have a tendency toward getting acne themselves.

If you do get a pimple, don't squeeze it. Popping pimples can spread bacteria and cause infection. This leads to increased redness, inflammation, and scarring of your skin. Your best bet? Wash your face and then apply an over-the-counter acne medication that contains benzoyl peroxide or salicylic acid. A dermatologist can provide you with acne care tips and a stronger, prescription medicine if necessary. If you are careful to keep your skin clean, eat well (not too many greasy foods!), and not get too stressed out, you should be able to keep any acne problem that develops during your teen years under control.

Safe from the sun

Believe it or not, in most cases ninety percent of sun damage to the skin is done before the age of twenty! How you treat your skin today can have long-lasting results.

Sunburns cause the worst damage to your skin, and they occur more often to those people who have fair or pale skin. Scary as it may seem, one serious sunburn can cause irreparable damage. What's more, sun exposure has been shown to cause skin cancer, a potentially deadly disease — and one that's showing up in younger and younger patients.

Your best protection against the sun: Wear a good sunscreen anytime you're outdoors . . . no matter what the weather or where you are. The harmful UVA and UVB rays that cause cancer cut through cloud cover and can do damage regardless of the temperature outside (and whether or not the sun is shining).

Sunscreens are rated according to their sun

protection factor, or SPF. An SPF of 15 means that it will protect you up to 15 times longer and better than if you weren't wearing any sunscreen. Wearing a sunscreen with an SPF of 15 will allow you to stay burn-free for up to 150 minutes, or two and a half hours. Sunscreen should be reapplied after swimming or vigorous exercise.

No tan is a healthy tan. A tan is your body's way of trying to protect your skin from too much sun exposure. It also speeds up your skin's aging process. If you're really longing to have a little color, consider a sun-free self-tanning lotion instead. It'll give you the color you crave and save your skin from sun damage.

Detecting your type

Is your skin oily, dry, or somewhere in between? Knowing your skin type will enable you to care for it properly. Check out the descriptions below to determine your skin type.

Oily skin: This type of skin produces more oil than is necessary. The oil can cause your face to get shiny during the day. Humid conditions can make it shinier. Oily skin tends to be more prone to pimples. It's best to wash your face several times a day if you have oily skin. *The test:* Wipe a tissue across your face after school. If there's an oily residue on it, your skin could be oily. *Oily skin benefit:* As they age, people with oily skin usually get fewer wrinkles!

Normal skin: This type of skin is neither too dry nor too oily. Normal skin only requires the most basic of skin-care routines: Wash twice a day with a facial cleanser formulated for normal skin. The test: If your skin doesn't feel tight and doesn't show a shine after school, your skin is likely to be normal. *Normal skin benefit:* You don't have to worry about major acne problems or premature aging when you're older.

Dry skin: This type of skin doesn't produce enough oils. It can feel tight after washing with soap so it's best to use a mild cleanser instead. Dry skin may develop rough, scaly patches in dry or cold weather and require occasional moisturizer. *The test:* Does your skin feel tight after you wash it or are you prone to dry patches? If so, your skin may be dry. *Dry skin benefit:* Preteens or teens with dry skin don't have to worry about having a shiny face or an acne breakout.

Combination skin: This type of skin is when certain areas (like the forehead, nose, and chin) are high on oil-production, while other areas (like cheeks) produce just the right amount. The "T-zone" — the forehead, nose, and chin area — is usually acne-prone while your cheeks may need some moisturizer. *The test:* If your skin seems shiny in the T-zone but normal to dry in other areas, your skin could be combination. *Combination skin benefit:* Like with normal skin, people with combo skin probably will manage to avoid most serious skin problems associated with oily skin.

Weather warning

Mother Nature can wreak havoc on your skin. Just when you think you have skin care under control, a change of season can come along and really throw things off. Or, during a visit to your grandparents in Florida, you could find that your skin ends up reacting pretty strangely. That's because the air is not only different at different times of the year but in different climates also.

In many regions, winter weather brings cold, dry air. Your skin may feel dry and tight during these months, so you might want to use a moisturizer (or a soap with moisturizer) to keep dry skin at a minimum. Using warm water to wash, instead of hot water, can also help. In other climates, like the desert or the mountains, the weather can be dry year-round, and your skin may crave extra moisture. Even though it may be warm, the lack of moisture in the air can require some extra skin care.

In the summer, winds from the south carry moisture north. They often bring warm, humid weather to much of the region east of the Rocky Mountains, and all the way north to Canada. This humid, moist weather keeps normal to dry skin feeling supple but can exacerbate an oily skin problem. If you have oily skin, you may need to use a stronger soap or a toner or astringent to keep shiny skin under control.

Beauty myths

Not all you hear about beauty is true; some stories are just plain tall tales. Here's the real buzz on some beauty myths.

Myth: Eating chocolate causes pimples.
Reality: Poor old chocolate has been getting a bad rap for ages. Singled out, chocolate does not cause breakouts (unless of course you're allergic to it, which is a completely different

story). The truth in this tale is that eating a diet that's high in sweets and fatty foods and low in nutrition (chocolate has loads of sugar, calories, and fat) can take a toll on your skin. Eating a well-balanced diet — which can certainly include the occasional chocolate chip cookie or candy bar — and getting proper rest will help keep your skin looking its best.

Myth: You can't get sunburned in the winter.
Reality: Even when it's stuck behind nasty storm clouds or when the air is cold, the sun is still there all year long, casting its harmful rays in our direction. Skiers or snowboarders who fail to realize this can wind up with a pretty nasty burn if they aren't careful. If you plan on going outside — whether rain, shine, snow, or sleet — wear sunscreen.

Myth: Licking your lips will keep them moist.
Reality: Licking your lips will actually dry them out. That's because wetting your lips with your tongue causes dehydration . . . meaning they'll wind up becoming even more dry and chapped. The best treatment for sore, chapped lips? Apply a lip balm.

Myth: Squeezing a pimple makes it disappear faster.

Reality: Putting the squeeze on a pimple can make the problem worse by causing infection and even scarring. When it comes to blemishes, adopt a hands-off policy.

Myth: Brushing your hair one hundred strokes each night will make it shiny.

Reality: All that brushing will just make you tired! The thought behind this myth was that brushing stimulates the oils in your scalp, which help to give your hair a glow. Not so! The amount of oil you'll stimulate won't be enough to do any serious shine work. And even if it did, your hair would look oily, not shiny! Your best bet for shiny hair is to keep your tresses clean and to use a conditioner or styling aid that promotes shine.

Myth: Rubbing a lemon on your skin will make freckles disappear.

Reality: While the acidic lemon does have some bleaching ability, it won't get rid of your freckles, so save your lemons for making lemonade! Some freckles are hereditary — which means you inherited them. Other freckles come as a result of too much exposure to the sun. You can help prevent these sun spots from showing up by wearing a sunscreen when you're outdoors. But why try and banish your natural freckles? Show them off instead — they're as cute as can be!

Myth: You can't get sunburned in the pool.
Reality: No sunscreen while swimming? Ouch! You can most definitely get sunburned while taking a dip. At least half of the sun's rays easily make their way through water. If you're going to hit the H_2O, wear a waterproof sunscreen and be sure to apply it at least fifteen minutes before you take the plunge to allow it time to dry.

Myth: Scrubbing your face with a facial scrub will give your skin a healthy glow.
Reality: If you use a facial scrub, a product that's intended to remove the dry or dead skin from the surface, be sure it's gentle enough for your skin. And since the ingredients in the product already act as a scrub, all you need to do is gently massage or pat the product on your skin. To avoid a red face, test a small area on your face first.

Lip service

Your lips are highly vulnerable to the elements because they have thinner skin and are more sensitive and therefore have less natural protection from direct sunlight than the skin on the rest of your body.

You can combat dry, chapped lips by using lip balm. Pick your flavor — lip balms come in so many yummy ones. If you plan to be in the sun, choose a lip balm that contains sunscreen.

Another lip product is lip gloss, which provides more shine than it does protection. You can find lip glosses in assorted flavors as well, and some also have a slight hint of color. Take your pick of tub-style, which you apply with your fingers, or tube-style, which you apply to the lips with its applicator.

Nail care know-how

Want a perfect 10? Here are some tips for knockout nails.

Cleaning: Dirt gets trapped easily under fingernails. So while washing your hands is usually enough to keep your nails clean, on occasion you may need to use a nailbrush and scrub underneath your nails with soap and water. The tip of an orange stick — a slender wooden tool designed for cuticle and nail care — can also be used to dislodge the dirt hiding underneath your nails.

Filing: Using a nail file will keep your nails looking even and well-shaped. Don't use a nail file like a saw. Instead, file back and forth gently, rounding off at the corners.

Giving 'em the clip: To keep your nails trim, use nail clippers and cut straight across the nail. Don't try to shape your nails with the clippers — use a nail file for any fancy nail work. Toenails especially require regular clipping to keep them at a comfortable length.

Cuticle care: The cuticle is the delicate skin at the base of your fingernail. Proper care means keeping cuticles pushed back from the nail beds. Use an orange stick to gently push cuticles back. Avoid clipping the skin from this fragile area because that can cause irritation and even infections.

Ridges: Those little ridges on your nails are nothing to worry about. They could be due to a damaged nail, or simply could be a characteristic of your nails. You can usually give ridges the rub with a nail buffer.

Damaged nails: Cracking, peeling, and brittle nails are often caused by a lack of moisture. Cold weather, or exposing your nails to excessive amounts of hot water and harsh soaps, can make these conditions even worse. Protect your nails by applying a moisturizing lotion (there are some specially formulated for hand and nail care) frequently during the day or by using a nail hardener. You can make damaged nails less obvious by smoothing rough edges with a nail file.

Yellow nails: Nail polish sometimes leaves a yellow tint on your nails after it's removed, especially if you wear a dark color. Your best defense is to apply a clear base coat to keep the color from coming into direct contact with your nails. To remove these color stains, wipe nails with a cotton ball that's been soaked with rubbing alcohol.

Nail biting: Biting your nails really . . . well, bites. Besides leaving you with gross-looking nails, it also makes you appear nervous and self-conscious. It's a bad and unsightly habit that's tough to break, but keeping your nails manicured can help. If your nails look pretty, you'll be less tempted to chomp on them. If rough edges are an invitation for you to start nibbling on your nails, keep a file on hand to smooth them out.

No-fail nails

There's no need to visit a salon to get your nails looking great: With just a few tools and a few minutes, you can give yourself an at-home manicure in no time.

What You Need:
Nail polish remover
Cotton balls or pads
Bowl of warm, soapy water
Nail file
Pair of nail clippers
Orange stick
Moisturizing lotion
Clear base coat
Nail polish
Clear top coat

What You Do:

1. File: It's best to file your nails first, before you soften them in the warm, soapy water. Give yourself rounded nails, or file straight across the top to form a squared look. If the length of your nails is uneven, consider clipping the long ones to the length of your shorter nails.

2. Clean: Remove any old polish residue from your nails using a cotton ball dipped in nail polish remover. Then soak your nails in the warm, soapy water for about five minutes to soften them. Dry your nails after you've finished.

3. Push back: Using the flat end of an orange stick, gently push back your cuticles. If your cuticles are out of control, try using a cuticle cream.

4. Moisturize: Use a specially formulated nail-care lotion and massage into your hands and nails. This will make your nails more supple and less prone to breaking. Wipe away any excess lotion.

5. Clear: Clear away any residue from the tops of your nails or else your polish won't stay put.

6. Paint: Start with a clear base coat, which will help nail color last longer and prevent your nails from becoming stained. Let the base coat dry, then apply your color of choice. Put on one to two coats of color. To correct polish mistakes, dip the pointy end of an orange stick in nail polish remover and gently wipe away unwanted color. Finish with a clear, fast-drying top coat, and allow plenty of time for your nails to dry. (Note: You can use the same clear polish as both your base coat and top coat.)

Out-of-the-ordinary nails

When you're in the mood for something different, try these novel nail-care options.

- Nail decals are fresh, fun, and easy to apply. You can find nail art at a drugstore or beauty supply store. While some types require a special glue to affix them to the top of your nails, others attach easily. Choose from jewels, stickers, or even your name or initials.

- Glittered polish gives your nails sparkle and shine and is perfect for special occasions. Go for glitter that's premixed with your color choice, or apply a clear polish containing glitter over nails that have already been painted.

- Nail polish color choices are endless and anything but boring. Try fun and funky colors like purple, blue, and lime green, or opt for some extra glitz with shades like bronze, copper, silver, or gold. If soft is more your style, pick pastels, like a soft pink or even just plain white or beige.

Servicing your smile

Your teeth take center stage far too often for you to ignore them. When you smile, talk, or eat, your teeth are sure to be noticed. Give them the dental attention they deserve and they can be one of your best beauty assets.

Brusha, brusha, brusha

Not to gross you out, but your mouth is full of bacteria that like to feed on whatever food they find trapped in your mouth. The by-product of this bacteria feeding frenzy is plaque that rests on your teeth. Too much of this can lead to tooth decay and cavities.

You can annihilate the acid, as well as food particles, bacteria, and the stains that accumulate on the surface of your teeth, with fluoride. Brush your teeth with a toothpaste containing fluoride at least twice a day — in the morning after you eat breakfast and at night after dinner or before you go to bed.

When you brush, think about vibrating, not sawing, and direct the bristles of the brush away from your gum line. Establish a brushing pattern that feels comfortable to you: like first brushing your upper teeth, then the back, then the lowers. It takes at least a minute to cover all surfaces of your teeth. Be sure to brush on the gum line, too, where food often gets lodged.

Your best brush bet is one with soft or medium bristles. Firm or hard bristles are too abrasive and can do a number on your gums. Pick a toothbrush with a small-sized head — essential for reaching those all-the-way-back places. And be sure to replace your toothbrush every three months because by then it's worn-out. Or if you get sick, replace your toothbrush once you're better to get rid of the germs.

Flossing is really the only way to get rid of plaque and food particles from between your teeth. Once a day at least (although it's preferable to floss after each meal), take some dental floss and insert it in each space between two teeth and gently scrape the floss up and down against the side of both teeth.

What you eat can affect your dental health as well. The worst offenders are sugary or sticky foods, which get stuck in the grooves of your teeth and are hard to get out. Seemingly innocent raisins are cavity culprits, as are dried fruits and sticky candies such as caramels and taffy. Also on the dental hit list: soda, which quickly and easily breaks down into the acids that cause tooth decay. It's best to avoid eating these decay-causing foods right before bed, since any particles you aren't able to remove (and brushing and flossing never get rid of *everything*) have all night to become the bacteria's prey without the benefit of the extra saliva your mouth produces during the day to wash them away. If you can't brush your teeth immediately after eating sticky or sweet food, at least rinse your mouth thoroughly with water.

Brushing, flossing, and watching what and when you eat aren't your only defenses against tooth decay. Twice a year, pay a visit to the dentist's office for a cleaning and a checkup. If your dentist spots a cavity forming, a fluoride treatment can help combat it.

Hey, brace-face!

Between the ages of two and twelve, your baby teeth are slowly coming out and making room for the teeth you'll hang onto — hopefully — for the rest of your life. Whether or not these new teeth will come in straight has to do with how much room they have in which to maneuver. If a permanent tooth starts coming in before the baby tooth has fallen out, it will sometimes end up coming in crooked. Your mouth may also just not have enough room to fit the larger set of permanent teeth. Hence the need for braces.

Even before all of your adult teeth arrive, though, your dentist can decide to send you in for preorthodontic work. This will help to lessen the need for braces or cut down on the time you'll spend wearing them. By making room for a mouth full of permanent teeth, there's a better chance they'll come in straight.

If you do need braces, though, don't fret. Gone are the days when braces meant a mouth full of uncomfortable metal. Today you can get small-sized braces, braces worn behind your teeth, or even removable ones. Ask your orthodontist about your options.

If you do wear braces, be sure to take extra care in keeping your teeth clean — unless you want a permanent reminder of your time spent in braces! Be sure to focus on the area near the gum line, where food can become lodged.

Chapter Two
Hair Care

Let's face it: Having great-looking hair can be a little high-maintenance. It's not enough just to keep it clean and conditioned. You also need to keep the ends healthy through regular trims. Find a style that makes sense for you, then deal with daily styling and drying.

This chapter will take you through the steps you need to keep your hair looking its best. You'll learn all about caring for your hair, finding a style that's right for you, and coming up with the right tools to get the look you'll love.

Tress TLC

Keeping your tresses in tip-top shape requires cleaning, conditioning, and regular maintenance. Check out these tried-and-true tress tips to leave yours looking its best.

- Use a shampoo that's formulated for your hair type. Apply a small amount to your hands — you'll need enough to create a lather — then rub it into your hair, starting at the scalp. Since oil is produced at the scalp, concentrate on sudsing up on top first, then working your way to the ends. Use the tips of your fingers to gently massage your head and scalp. Rinse thoroughly, as shampoo residue can cause dryness.
- Once a month try using a different shampoo for a week. Hair tends to get used to a particular formula when you use it over and over and it can end up becoming less effective. By using something new you give your hair a rest.
- You might not need to shampoo every day. Shampooing strips the hair of its natural oils, so if your hair is dry, twice a week may do it for you. However, if you have oily hair you'll probably find washing every day to be necessary to ward off the greasies.
- If you don't have oily hair, apply a conditioner. Concentrate the conditioner in the areas that need it most, which will likely be the ends. If you have superdry hair, try a deep-conditioning treatment about once a month. Leave-on conditioners that you

apply after you wash can provide added repair and protection against drying and styling.

- Comb wet hair with a wide-toothed comb to help prevent breakage. Start at the ends (you don't want your hair broken at the crown), then finish at the roots.

- Split ends are caused by overly drying or styling hair. While you can minimize the look of damaged ends, you can't repair them. It's important to go easy on hot-air styling to prevent split ends. Also get your hair trimmed regularly to keep away damaged ends and help your hair look its healthy best.

- Try blow-drying your hair from the top down to give it extra body and lift. Turn your head upside down and dry the roots first. Then flip your head back over and blow-style the ends.

Salon speak

You can take the trauma out of getting a trim by learning how to find and communicate with a stylist.

Finding a stylist: It's important to trust your stylist, and the best way to find someone you can trust is to go on recommendations. Ask a friend whose hairstyle you like and who has hair like yours to give you the name of her stylist.

Go for a consultation: Many stylists will spend time with you before you go in for the actual cut in order to find out what you have in mind and to suggest styles for you. This is the best time to say specifically what you want and to get a feel as to whether the stylist understands what you are asking for. If you're unsure about the style you want, the stylist can show you some shots from hair books as examples. Or another great way to be sure you'll get the cut you want is to bring in photos from magazines of styles you'd like to try.

Speak your worries: What are your concerns about getting a haircut? Are you worried your stylist will cut off too much, give you unwanted bangs, or do something too extreme? Be sure to speak your mind before he or she brings out the scissors. Be as specific as you can about what you want. "Just a trim" to him may mean an inch, but to you it could mean a quarter of an inch. Before your stylist cuts off any length, ask him to show you where he plans to cut. Speak up before it's too late if he's planning to cut too much. You'll also want to find out how much maintenance your new style requires. If you're used to wash-'n'-go hair, that new layered do that requires drying, curling, and a ton of styling aids may not be your best bet.

Go slow: If you are uneasy about going from long to short, get there slowly by getting your hair cut in steps, and taking off a little more each time you visit the salon. That way, if you don't like it, you won't have to wait for ages for it to grow back.

Ask questions: A new style is of no use to you if you can't duplicate the look at home. Ask your stylist how she is styling the new look — and what tools or styling aids you will need to create the look by yourself.

Help for your hair type

Knowing your hair's characteristics can make it much easier for you to care for and style it. Here's how to figure out your type, then find the products that will keep it looking its best.

If your hair . . .
- seems thin
- gets weighted down by styling aids
- dries naturally straight and smooth

. . . you have fine hair. You need products made specially for fine hair that will add body. You can give fine hair a boost by blow-drying it with your head held upside down. A layered cut can also help add body and bounce.

If your hair . . .
- tends to tangle easily
- is prone to the frizzies
- seems thick or coarse

. . . you have flyaway or dry hair. You need to restore lost moisture to your hair. Use a conditioning shampoo, as well as a conditioner, each time you wash to control the flyaways. Watch out for styling aids that contain alcohol, which can be drying. Excess heat from styling tools like a blow-dryer or curling iron can contribute to the frizzies. Why not go natural by letting your hair dry on its own?

If your hair . . .
- looks oily by the end of the day, even if you wash it in the morning

• gets dry on the ends, but not on the scalp . . . you have oily hair. Fight the greasies by shampooing daily and only applying conditioner to the areas that need it. Avoid using an excess of styling aids, which can weigh down your hair and make it appear even oilier. You might want to consider a style that keeps hair off your face, since oil from your face can get on your hair and weigh it down even more.

If your hair . . .
• gets split ends easily
• lacks shine
• seems unhealthy, especially after you blow-dry it

. . . you have hair that's likely damaged. Since your locks are lacking moisture, it's no wonder your hair looks a little dull. Revive those tired tresses by first getting the ends trimmed. Then use a deep-conditioning treatment to help put the shine back in your style. And watch out for your surroundings: Hair gets damaged by things like wind, excessive use of heated styling products, and chlorine when you swim.

Curly, straight, or somewhere in between?

If you were to let your hair dry naturally, how would it look? Do you have a ton of tight curls, a few big waves, or is your hair straight as a ruler? Here are some styling tips that'll make the most of your hair type.

Curly hair: Girls with curls too often try to straighten their hair. Curls are cute and desirable — why do you think so many people pay for perms? — so show them off with style. Either let curly hair dry naturally or use a diffuser attachment on a blow-dryer and scrunch sections of hair as you dry. Short, long, and shoulder-length styles all look good with your type of hair, so pick your preference and let your curls shine through.

Wavy hair: Adding layers to wavy hair will give you more body and allow you to flaunt big, bouncy waves. You can make waves appear even curlier by using a gel and scrunch-drying your hair. If you prefer softer waves, blow-dry your hair using a round brush until it is damp. Then let it dry completely on its own. Wavy hair is perfect for holding curls, so try using a large curling iron or hot rollers for added body and curl on special occasions.

Straight hair: While you may get superfrustrated watching curls fall out of your hair, straight, healthy hair shows off shine better than any other type. Be proud of your luscious locks! Blunt ends are best for straight hair, as layers may appear choppy. If long hair seems to weigh you down, add bangs or go for a cropped-at-the-shoulders cut. Or ask your stylist to taper the sides to frame your face.

The best do for your face shape

Your hair is what frames your face. Depending on the shape of your face, certain styles are going to provide the best frame. So the first step to finding the perfect hairstyle to flatter your face is to determine whether your face shape is round, oval, square, long, or heart-shaped. Here's a surefire way to figure it out:

Pull your hair back off your face and stand in front of a mirror. Using a bar of soap or lipstick (or another writing instrument that can wipe easily off the mirror), draw an outline on the mirror around the reflection of your face. Step away and examine your drawing. Is it squared-off near the jaw? If so, you have a square-shaped face. Is your face drawing oval or egg-shaped, or more round or oblong? If it's round on the sides but thin toward the chin, you have a heart-shaped face. Once you know your face shape, read on for the styles that are right for you.

Oval face: Lots of styles will work for you. Try your hair long or somewhere in between. Go curly or stay straight. Find a cut that suits you. If you're an on-the-go girl, you'll want a wash-and-go cut, or one that you can easily put up in a ponytail. Keep your hair type in mind as well. If you have ultrathick hair, you may find it much more manageable in a short do than worn long.

Round face: Mid-length or shoulder-length hair works wonderfully on girls with round faces. Watch out for too-short styles, which can overemphasize the roundness of your face. And if you opt for bangs, try them soft, wispy, and not too blunt. If you want to elongate your face (so it won't seem as round), try parting your hair on the side and giving it a little lift up top. Straight hair or soft waves are the top texture for your style.

Long face: Bangs are the best for long-faced gals — they'll make your face look perfectly proportioned. Chin-length or shoulder-length hair works well, and if you choose to go long, try adding soft layers around your face. Curls and waves are right for you, and a side part will make any style you wear look best.

Square face: Face-framing layers will show off your cheekbones without making your face appear boxy. Since your face shape is so defined, you'll want to keep your cut and curls soft. Try waves, wisps, or curls. If you're bold, why not brave it and try a short style? It'll no doubt look awesome on you!

Heart-shaped face: You'll want fullness near the jawline to help balance your features. Try curls or waves that begin below your ears. Chin- or shoulder-length hair is best for you, but if you love long locks, try adding extra curls or waves on the ends or gentle layers that begin below the ears. A sassy, flipped-up shoulder-length do would look great on you!

Product glossary

Should you go for the goop or make a play for the mousse? Check out the info below to figure out what styling aids make the most sense for you.

Gel

What it does: Gives your hairstyle long-lasting hold and adds extra shine when applied to wet hair. When used on dry hair, it gives your hair that ultraslick look.

Best for: Hair that already has a little lift, as gel won't necessarily add body. If you have dry hair, it's best to choose an alcohol-free gel to avoid overdrying your hair. Beware of clumping, which is caused by using too much gel.

How to use: Pick the best gel for your hair type according to the package labels, then place a small amount in your hand. For short hair, use about a dime-sized dollop. For medium hair, try a teaspoonful, and for long hair, use about a teaspoon and a half. Apply to either wet or dry hair, then style as usual.

Mousse

What it does: Helps add body and fullness to your hair. Will add hold without causing clumps or stickiness.

Best for: Dry or flat hair that needs extra body, but if your hair is superthick or coarse, you may find that even the lightest of mousses will weigh your hair down.

How to use: Place a dollop about the size of a golf ball (you may need more if your hair is longer) in your palm. Lightly rub your palms with the mousse, then run both hands through your wet hair, applying the mousse evenly. Blow-dry or style as usual.

Pomade or laminating gel

What it does: Adds extra shine and texture to your hair. When used on wet hair, can add flexible body to the hair.

Best for: Dry or normal hair, but if you use too much, beware of getting greasy clumps in your hair. If you already have oily hair, pomade or laminating gel may cause your hair to appear greasier.

How to use: Apply a very small amount to the palm of your hand. Rub your palms together, then distribute evenly through either damp or dry hair.

Heat-activated hair treatment

What it does: Provides hair protection for heat-styling your hair. Can help condition overly styled hair.

Best for: Dry or damaged hair. But don't think a heat protectant gives you the green light to go hog-wild with the blow-dryer — these products won't provide complete protection. They also won't repair things like split ends. It's still best to get regular trims to take care of tired ends.

How to use: Spray on a small amount to wet or damp hair before you blow-dry, then style as usual.

Hair spray or finishing spritz

What it does: Helps hold your style in place. Can keep curls from falling, or add body when applied to the roots. Good for helping fine, flyaway hair.

Best for: All types of hair. Don't go overboard applying hair spray or your hair will feel stiff and dry. Unless you're trying to keep an up do up, look for a light hold for everyday use.

How to use: Lightly spritz or spray dry, styled hair. Unless the product says otherwise, for maximum hold, avoid brushing hair after you've applied hair spray.

Tools of the trade

You just need to visit the hair-care aisle at the beauty supply or grocery store to realize that there are a ton of gizmos and gadgets to use on your hair. Among brushes alone, your options are endless! Before you go out and try to rack up an arsenal of hair tools, take a look at what each does.

Round brush: Rounded brushes are great for adding waves and curls while you blow-dry. For longer hair, choose a larger-barreled brush. To use, wrap strands of hair around the brush as you blow-dry. Don't hold the dryer over one section of your hair for too long, though, as you don't want to burn or dry out your hair.

Vent brush: Vent brushes can add body to your hair while you're blow-drying. Just lift and pull strands of hair with the vent brush as you dry. A vent brush also cuts down on the time needed to blow-dry your hair, since it allows the air to flow through.

Paddle brush: A paddle brush has a large face that's perfect for keeping long locks in place. Choose one with nylon or wire bristles to help get through thick hair.

Natural- or boar-bristle brushes: These are great for thin or fine hair since the bristles won't have a tough time getting through to your scalp. For that reason, they're not the best choice for thick hair.

Blow-dryers: Blow-dryers aren't just for drying hair — they're a great styling aid as well. For best blow-styling results, section off your hair and blow-dry one section at a time, using a round brush or vent brush. When your hair is nearly dry, you can use large Velcro rollers to add extra body and waves. For curly or wavy styles, use a diffuser attachment on your blow-dryer, then scrunch hair as you blow-dry. Or if you want to add curl while you dry, opt for a hot-air brush — a dryer with a brush attached to it. Use the cool button to finish off. Cool air will close your pores, which the heat opened, and help set the style.

Curling irons: Curling irons can add curl to straight hair or straighten out unwanted waves. You can select from small irons, which result in small ringlet curls, or large irons, which add body and big curls, or somewhere in between. Some curling irons have brush bristles attached to the wand, which create looser curls and add body. To create curls, wrap sections of hair around the curling iron. Hold for just a few seconds, then release the hair. Let your locks cool for a minute before you brush them. If you want to straighten hair, slowly pull the curling iron through a strand of hair, starting from the roots.

Straightening iron: This is a great tool for girls with frizzy or extremely curly hair. It has a much larger head than a regular curling iron, and the iron is flat.

Hot rollers: Heated rollers produce long-lasting curls. Just get them heated and roll sections of your hair in the direction you'd like the curls (for instance, if you want to flip your hair in the back, roll your hair upward). Let your hair set in the rollers for five to ten minutes, then remove. For tighter curls, let your hair cool before brushing. For looser curls, style your hair immediately after you remove the rollers using your brush of choice. If it's body you crave, supersize your set with jumbo-sized rollers.

Chapter Three
Body Beautiful

Your good looks don't stop at the neck. Taking care of the rest of your body — from the inside out — is equally important in your good grooming routine. That's why this chapter focuses on making your body look and feel beautiful — everything from eating right to exercising to proper hygiene.

Fueling your machine

Good looks really aren't just skin-deep. How you take care of the inside of your body is an essential part of your beauty regimen. Case in point: When you feel sick on the inside, it's usually pretty evident on the outside. Staying active and eating a healthy, well-balanced diet will not only make you feel better about yourself, it'll also make you look better.

Loading up on junk food and not getting the nutrients you need can make your skin seem sallow and your hair listless and make you feel energy-less, too. To be sure you're getting the vitamins and minerals you need, the majority of the foods you eat should be fruits and vegetables; breads, cereal, rice, and pasta; and proteins like meat, fish, milk and other dairy products like cheese and yogurt, and nuts. Limit your intake of fats and oils. Limit sweets, too, which have little to no nutritional value and only contribute empty calories.

You don't need to go nutso, though, trying to count your servings. In fact, you'd be surprised at how easy it is to get the nutrition you need to stay healthy — you're probably already getting lots of vitamins and nutrients from the foods you already eat on a regular basis. Just take a look at the sample diet on the following page, which contains at least the minimum amount of servings from each food group (as recommended by doctors and nutritionists) but yet doesn't go overboard in any one area. You'll probably agree that eating healthily doesn't have to mean being stuck eating gross foods.

Breakfast
Bowl of cereal with milk
Glass of orange juice
Banana

Snack
Celery slices topped with peanut butter

Lunch
Turkey sandwich with cheese, lettuce,
tomato, and mayonnaise
Apple

Snack
Frozen yogurt with fresh strawberries

Dinner
Pasta with tomato sauce and sliced
mushrooms
Salad with dressing
Dinner roll

Rate your diet

To figure out whether you're getting the nutrients you need on a regular basis, keep a food
diary for a few days. Write down everything
that you eat each day, then take a closer look.

Are you skimping in a certain area and going overboard in others? Figure out where you need to modify your diet — it means cutting down on sweets and fats and upping your intake of fruits and vegetables. Once you figure out your nutritional pitfalls, change your diet to include the foods you need. In no time, you'll begin to notice that you feel more energized and your skin looks healthier, too!

Why it's not smart to diet

Unless your doctor recommends it, dieting is bad for your health, your looks, and your attitude! Food is energy — your body needs nutrients to keep all of its parts functioning properly. When you start to limit your food intake or cut out certain foods, you reduce the amount of important and vital nutrients your body gets. Your energy level will go down, as will your metabolism. Eating a well-balanced diet and staying active will automatically keep your body at its ideal shape.

Diet dos: Tips for a healthier diet

1. Practice smart snacking. Your mom and dad may do a great job keeping meals healthful —

but all those cookies and candy bars between meals can really mess things up for you. Instead, keep a stash of healthy snacks on hand, like fresh fruit, vegetables, or cereal bars. That way, you'll be less tempted to splurge on nutrient-deficient snacks like candy bars and cookies.

2. Avoid too much soda. Sugared soda may provide a quick boost of sugar energy, but it won't give you long-lasting energy, nor will it satisfy your thirst. Plus sodas (even diet sodas) can contribute to tooth decay and cavities. Be smart and stick with water!

3. Listen to your body. Eat when you are hungry and stop when you are full. Hunger is a sign that your body needs nutrients. Don't deprive yourself!

4. Don't be a junk-food junkie. Many times it's not the food at a junk-food joint that's bad for you, it's the method of preparation. Look at burgers: They have your basic protein, vegetables, and bread. But not all hamburger meat is lean, and frying up a burger isn't exactly the low-fat way to prepare it. And french fries may start out as potatoes, but by the time they make it into your Combo Meal #3, they're anything but healthy! If you do hit the fast-food stands often, look for more healthful selections, like grilled chicken sandwiches, low-fat shakes, and salads.

5. Be brown-bag smart. Don't bag good eating habits just because you bring your lunch to school. Instead, fill your sack with a healthy midday meal. Some to consider:

- Tuna sandwich on wheat bread; fruit yogurt; pretzels; and milk
- Ham and cheese sandwich with lettuce, tomato, and mayonnaise; baked potato chips; and a fruit drink
- Peanut butter and jelly sandwich; fruit juice; and low-fat chocolate pudding
- Crackers with cold cuts and cheese; carrot sticks; and orange juice

6. Make time for breakfast. Breakfast is the most important meal of the day. Skip it and you'll likely feel lethargic all morning and famished by lunch. Even if you're pressed for time, don't try to get through the morning without something in your stomach. Grab a breakfast bar to go, or take along fruit on your commute to class.

Playtime

Couch potatoes beware: Studies show that staying active can make you feel better. Even just walking twenty minutes a day can change your outlook. And feeling good about yourself on the inside shows on the outside. You don't need to join an expensive gym to fit fitness into your life, though. Nor do you need to join a sports team that seems boring to you! There are so many fitness options to choose from; all you need to do is decide which works best for you.

Change your exercise attitude

Exercise might sound like a chore, but when you understand the many ways that "exercise" can be incorporated into your day, you'll see that staying fit can be fun. The important thing is to get your body in motion: Instead of sitting on the couch and watching TV on a Saturday afternoon, put on your skates and get outside! Here are some other ways to work a little activity into your life.

- **Walk to school instead of taking the bus:** If the weather's OK, opt to walk. You don't need any special gear, just your feet. What an easy way to get some exercise!

- **Go for a swim:** Doing some laps in the pool during the summer is a great way to work most of your muscle groups and get fit. You can also take part in other pool activities, like water volleyball, synchronized swim classes, or even diving for pool rings.
- **Play a game of volleyball at the beach:** Don't just sit in the sand and sunbathe — make your treks to the beach more active with a game of volleyball. Volleyball can be played with a group, or one-on-one if it's just you and a pal.
- **Go in-line skating:** In-line skating puts your legs to work and helps improve coordination. Falls can be dangerous, so be sure to wear the proper protection, including a helmet and knee, ankle, and elbow pads. Practice in an area that's free of hills and automobile traffic, like an empty parking lot or playground.
- **Take the stairs instead of the elevator:** Not even the stair climber can match the workout level of a good ole walk up the stairs.
- **Do your household chores:** Chores like vacuuming, dusting, and taking out the

garbage use much more energy than coming up with excuses as to why you didn't do them! Consider chore time another great way to get your body in motion.

- **Walk the dog:** Even Fido knows the importance of exercise, otherwise he wouldn't pull you away from your favorite TV show to take him for his daily walks. Instead of dreading this daily ritual, take advantage of being outdoors and enjoy the fresh air.

- **Try out a fitness trend, like yoga:** It may be trendy today, but yoga has been around for 5,000 years. Yoga encompasses not only your body but your mind and spirit as well. This ancient practice can help you achieve physical and mental health and tranquillity.

The sporting life

Joining a sport or activity class is a great way to make fitness a regular part of your life. If your school doesn't offer any extracurricular sports that appeal to you, check out the local YMCA. Most Ys offer fitness and dance classes or even swim leagues and sports teams. Check out the following options, and put an *x* next to the activities that interest you. Then determine how you can get involved: See which activities your school offers or ask your parents to help you find places to participate. It can be as easy as finding a friend to go walking or hiking with!

Aerobics
Ballet
Ballroom dancing
Baseball
Basketball
Bicycling
Bowling
Cheerleading
Cross-country skiing
Golf
Gymnastics
Hiking
Hockey
Horseback riding
Ice-skating
In-line skating or roller-skating
Jazz classes
Judo or karate
Modern dance
Ping-Pong
Racquetball
Running
Sailing

Skiing
Snowboarding
Soccer
Softball
Surfing
Swimming
Tap-dancing
Tennis
Volleyball
Walking
Weight training
Yoga

The wonders of water: Facts about this fabulous fluid

Drinking water is one of the best tricks of the beauty trade. Water hydrates your skin, prevents dehydration, and helps cleanse the body of toxins. So be sure to drink lots — at least eight glasses a day is what's recommended. Here's more information about nature's beauty secret:

- The human body consists of between forty and sixty percent water — and water helps keep your body functioning properly.

- Throughout the day, your body loses water. Sweating, moving around, even just breathing all cause your body to lose water.
- Most fruits and vegetables are packed with water, while foods like meat and bread have little water content. So be sure to eat lots of fruits and vegetables!
- Drinking caffeinated beverages, like colas or cappuccinos, can actually deplete your body of water because they're dehydrating.
- When it's hot out, or when you're involved in strenuous, sweat-producing activity, your body requires extra water.
- Your body may not always tell you when it's thirsty — by the time you actually feel thirsty it means you're already dehydrated. So make drinking water a habit, not something you do only when you're aware of being thirsty.

Bodycare basics from A to Z

Chances are, you don't live in a climate so cold you must stay covered up in heavy clothing all year. There are going to be times when you want to put on a pair of shorts or a cute dress to stay comfortable. And when you do, you'll feel much better if your skin is soft, smooth, clean, and clear. Keeping your skin in top shape is as easy as ABC . . . see for yourself!

Activity: Staying active will make your skin look radiant. Exercise gets the blood flowing. Be sure to fit fitness into your schedule.

Bathing: Taking a bath is not only a way to get clean, it's also a great way to relax.

Chlorine: It's in swimming pools and can dry out your skin. It's a good idea to take a quick shower and apply lotion, if necessary, after a swim.

Dry lips: Here's a tip to help chapped lips — apply a lip balm before you bathe or shower. The bathroom's moisture will help to lock in the emollients for smoother lips.

Exfoliating: Removing dead skin from your body will make your skin appear smoother. Use a loofah to gently rub away any dead surface skin.

Fragrance: Scent can be a great mood lifter! Using fragrant bath oils, lotions, or gels can help you smell (and feel) pretty all day.

Gels: Using a shower gel can often be gentler on your skin than bar soap.

Hot water: High water temperatures can dry out your skin. Keep the shower at lukewarm!

Insomnia: If you're having trouble falling asleep, take a warm bath. It can help relax you. Also try to clear your head of any stressful thoughts that could keep you tossing and turning. Sleep is crucial to your mental and physical well-being.

Jelly: Petroleum jelly is an inexpensive, multi-purpose beauty aid. Use it on chapped lips or apply it to cracked and dry skin. If you have dry, cracked heels, apply a thick layer of petroleum jelly and cover with socks before you go to bed. The next morning, your heels will feel smoother.

Knees, elbows, and feet: These body parts contain thicker skin than other parts of your body. You may need extra moisturizer in these dryness-prone areas.

Lotion: Applying lotion to your skin after a bath can help lock in the moisture, making your skin feel smooth and silky.

Mascara for hair: Temporary, washable hair mascara comes in a variety of fun and wild colors. You can easily add some highlights and streaks for parties or just when you're feeling a little adventurous.

Natural products: Some natural products can be just as effective, if not more effective, than the ones you find on the shelf at the drugstore. An oatmeal bath can help relieve the pain of sunburn.

Oils: Bath and body oils can add moisture to your skin. You can apply them either in the shower or bath, or to damp skin after you've finished showering.

Pamper yourself: Every once in a while do something extra special, whether it's getting a massage or taking a long bath. It'll make you feel great and relaxed.

Quiet time: Set aside at least fifteen minutes a day for time to yourself. Relaxation is an important part of a beauty routine.

Read the labels: With so many bath and beauty products on the market, it pays to read labels to be sure you're buying the product you need.

Sunscreen: It's not just your face that can be affected by the sun's rays. Use a sunscreen on all exposed areas of your body before going in the sun, and reapply often, especially after exercise or swimming.

Take care of yourself: You only have one body so treat it well. When you respect yourself enough to take care of yourself, other people will respect you, too.

Under-eye circles: These are often caused by a lack of sleep. Be sure you're getting at least eight hours a night! Drinking lots of water to stay hydrated helps, too.

Variety: Try out different bath products to find the one that's right for you. Don't be afraid to experiment.

Washcloths: These can be the best way to ex-foliate. Use them in the shower to help gently remove dead surface skin.

X-amine your skin: If you spot a mole or a mark that doesn't seem to go away, or that changes shape or color or gets bigger, alert your parents. You may want to have a derma-tologist check it out.

Young skin: Don't be fooled into thinking you need a ton of products and bath aids. Young skin needs far less than the skin of older adults. The younger you are, the more effi-cient your body is at producing the oils it needs. While it's fun to try sweet-smelling bath products, don't go overboard buying products you don't need!

Zzzzs: Most of us need at least eight hours of sleep each night. Without enough sleep, you'll feel irritable and your skin and hair will look dull and listless. Be sure to get your zzzs!

The at-home spa

You don't need big bucks to spend a day being pampered at a spa. You can create a luxurious day of total body bliss in your own home, by yourself or with a friend. Here's how:

Step One: Energize
You'll want to get the blood flowing in your body before you begin. Get your body in motion by taking a walk or doing some quick stretches.

Step Two: Scrub
Now it's time to buff your bod. Use a soft cloth to slough away any dead skin and leave your body feeling smooth. Pay extra attention to areas where your skin is thicker, such as your elbows, knees, and heels.

Step Three: Soak
Follow your body buffing with a relaxing soak in the tub. Add scented bath gel or salts to make your time in the tub even more relaxing. You may even want to keep a few scented candles near the tub. Once you're done bathing, apply body lotion to damp skin. Wrap yourself up in your favorite fluffy robe and get ready for step four.

Step Four: Facial

Pull your hair back using clips or a ponytail holder. Wash your face using a gentle soap or skin cleanser. Next prepare a soothing facial treatment by adding herbal tea bags to a bowl of warm water. Lean your face over the bowl and let it steam for a few minutes. Pat your face dry when finished.

Step Five: Relax

Turn on some soft, relaxing music, then kick back in a comfy chair, on a couch, or on your bed. Keep your feet elevated by placing a pillow underneath them. Close your eyes and take a few deep breaths. Free your mind of everyday thoughts and responsibilities including friends, homework, or chores — think about a favorite place or visualize your dreams. Relax for at least fifteen minutes — don't worry if you fall asleep! After the time is up, slowly stand and stretch your arms up. Take one last deep breath.

Fragrance facts

Get hold of the power of perfumes and fragrances. The sense of smell is a very strong one — scents can affect your mood and evoke memories — so don't neglect it! There are tons of beauty products available these days in a variety of scents, each with its own personality and effect. It's just a matter of putting your sniffer to the test to find the one you like best. But it's important to remember that any scent you wear should be very light. Overpowering scent is offensive to most people.

Finding your ideal scent

There are many different types of scents, from floral to fruity, musky to citrusy. Which type is right for you? Take this quick test to find your fragrance personality.

You prefer:
a. loose, flowery dresses.
b. jeans and activewear.
c. the latest styles.
d. sweater sets and classic clothing.

Your fave way to spend an afternoon?
a. reading and writing in your journal
b. playing sports

c. listening to the latest tunes from your favorite band
d. cuddled up on the couch, watching an old movie

The place that gives you peace is:
a. a quiet garden.
b. a swimming pool or gym.
c. a hustling, bustling mall.
d. a bookstore or coffeehouse.

If you chose mostly As, your fragrance style is romantic. Your best bets are soft and light floral fragrances. Because you like just a gentle hint of scent, a light lotion is your perfect fragrance pick.

If you chose mostly Bs, your style is active and on-the-go. You prefer sporty over sentimental, so be sure the scent you pick is fresh, not overwhelming. Cool, citrusy scents will keep you smelling great at rest or at play.

If you chose mostly Cs, you are trendy to the nth degree. You need something that's new and now — that you won't worry about switching when it goes out of style. From fun, offbeat scents like cola and tutti-frutti to more classic light colognes, you'll love to experiment with all the new scents. You can even try layering a few fragrances to create your own signature scent.

If you chose mostly Ds, your classic taste will keep you turning to the tried-and-true fragrances. You'll want products that have stood the test of time and that are elegant and somewhat understated. You've probably already raided your mom's scents, but why not venture out and find a fragrance that's really you?

Be scentsible!

1. When it comes to choosing a new fragrance, try before you buy. Scents smell differently on everyone. Visit the cosmetics counter and get a whiff of the way things smell in the bottle. When you find one you like, spritz some of it on your wrist. Then wait fifteen minutes and do a sniff test. It'll take the fragrance that long to react to your body's chemistry so you can really tell what it'll smell like on you.

2. Apply fragrance on your pulse points for long-lasting results. Your body heat is higher in these areas, meaning fragrance will come across stronger. Your pulse points include the inside of your wrists and behind your ears, elbows, and knees.

3. The best time to apply a scent? In the morning, after you've showered. Wait about fifteen minutes after you bathe or shower so that your body isn't too hot — otherwise, you'll wind up sweating off the scent before you leave the house.

4. Say no to scents before you play sports or take part in vigorous activities.

5. Don't go overboard on the aroma! You don't want your perfume to overpower you, so keep it light. Keep scents stored in a fairly cool environment. Heat can alter the smell of a fragrance, so be sure not to store products in direct sunlight.

6. Check out your aroma options. There are plenty of ways to scent up, so why not give some of these a try:

- **body oil:** Best applied while your skin is still damp, body oils provide long-lasting scent.
- **lotion:** For a light touch of fragrance, a scented lotion is your best bet.
- **all-over body spritz:** Spritzes add just a touch of scent.
- **scented soaps:** You'll wash away the dirt and be left smelling good.
- **bath oil:** It makes the bath-time experience even more luxurious and relaxing. Plus,

you'll have a hint of scent left on your body afterward.

- **scented shampoos and conditioners:** Because of the natural oils in your hair, scented hair products can give you long-lasting fragrance.
- **scented candles:** Why leave the power of perfume to just your body? Light a scented candle in your favorite fragrance and enjoy its soothing benefits.

Aromatherapy: Scents for the body and soul

Some scents don't just smell good — they can also affect the way you feel. Aromatherapy — the ancient art of using aromatic plants to help heal the mind, body, and spirit — puts the power of plants to work for you. Check out the aromatherapy guide below.

The chart below shows some of the scents commonly found on the market, along with their characteristics and benefits. You can find many of these scents in products like candles, bath oils, lotions, perfumes, and soaps.

Anise: This black-licorice scent is said to aid relaxation and restore emotional balance.

Chamomile: The soothing and toning qualities of chamomile can relax you and make you feel at ease. Used in tea, it can soothe you right to sleep!

Cinnamon: This scent evokes warmth and coziness. Maybe that's why this scent is so popular around the winter holidays.

Gardenia: The scent of gardenia is said to be mood-lifting. Wear a fragrance made with this great-smelling flower and you can't help but feel happy.

Lavender:  This versatile herb relaxes, soothes, restores and balances your body and mind. Depending on your body's needs, it'll either calm or stimulate. A drop of lavender oil on your pillow before bed is said to give you a peaceful night's sleep. You can also add a little to a tub of water to refresh tired feet.

Orange:

Invigorating orange refreshes and uplifts the spirit. It's also believed to brighten dull complexions. Just be sure not to use the real thing directly on your skin—look for it in lotions or oils.

Peppermint:

Cool peppermint is the perfect pick-me-up. It refreshes and uplifts the mind and body. It's known to aid digestion, so opt for peppermint tea after a meal. The aroma of peppermint can also revive you if you're feeling tired, so try a little peppermint oil when you need a homework boost! Spearmint has a similar effect.

Rosemary:

Rev up your mood with a little rosemary oil. The scent stimulates and soothes tired muscles. It'll also give you added concentration, so rub a little rosemary on before a big test.

Tea Tree Oil:

This mild-sounding oil is actually known for its powerful antiseptic qualities. It's said to help remedy acne, cold sores, warts, and burns.

Vanilla:

Sweet smelling vanilla oil is said to help you relax, but you don't need to raid the spice rack to find it. Vanilla's turning up in everything from perfume to soap to body lotion.

Posture pointers

Bet you never thought sitting up straight in your chair could be a simple but effective beauty trick. Believe it or not, your posture — the way you hold and carry your body — says a lot about you. If you have poor posture, slouch your shoulders, and walk with your head down, others might perceive you as lacking self-esteem or motivation. With good posture, you'll not only look good but feel good about yourself, too. The opposite is true for poor posture — it not only makes you look bad, it can make you feel bad, too. Since you're not holding the body in its most efficient position, you're more likely to feel strained or cause undue stress on your muscles and joints.

Good posture not only makes a much better impression on others, it is also kinder and gentler on your body. You'll feel more energetic because your muscles are working more efficiently. And when you sit, stand, and move properly, you'll look healthier, happier, and more self-confident. If you need a little primer on keeping your posture perfect, check out these tips.

Standing tall

When you stand, imagine that you're keeping a book balanced on your head. You'll have to keep your head up and your shoulders back to keep that book where it belongs! Concentrate on holding your stomach flat, with your ribs raised and your shoulders and head erect. Keep your knees straight but not locked (which can be mighty uncomfortable after a while and can also be bad for your knees). Practice standing in front of a mirror.

Walking proud

When you walk, walk tall. Keep your head up and your gaze straight ahead. Let your arms swing freely at your sides — folding them across your chest could make you appear withdrawn, unhappy, or angry.

Sitting tall

School chairs may not be the most comfortable things in the world, but sitting in them properly can make 'em just a little more cozy. Sit tall with both feet flat on the floor, keeping your back flat against the back of the chair and your head held up. If you need to lean forward to write at your desk, be sure you lean in straight — don't hunch forward.

Smiling — The best body language there is

A smile is much more than just a smile. When you smile, you appear happier, warmer, and more approachable. If you're at a social event where you don't know many people or are feeling uncomfortable, smiling will tell others that you are confident, comfortable, and approachable. Smiles can also make others feel better, so try to give a big grin to someone who looks like they could use a little cheering up . You'll be surprised how much of an effect it has. Make the effort to answer the phone smiling — even though the other person can't see you, they'll hear your smile in your voice. People are just naturally drawn to a happy face — and a happy person — so show off your smile every chance you get!

Chapter Four
Fashion Workshop

Fashion isn't just about keeping up with the trends or wearing the latest new looks — it's about expressing your own personal style. Selecting clothes that you feel comfortable wearing makes you feel more confident, and there's nothing that enhances your looks more than confidence!

This chapter is all about finding your unique look, one that blends the colors and styles that suit you best with your own personal preferences. You'll learn secrets to shopping that will save you both time and money. And there's also helpful information on how to build your wardrobe, starting with the basics.

Finding the look that's right for you

Discovering the colors and styles that look best on you — and that you feel best wearing — can save you lots of time and spare you from buying things that wind up wasting away in your closet unworn. Based on your coloring, your body type, and your taste, you can create a wardrobe that's just right for you!

Homing in on your best hues

Finding the best colors for your unique hair and skin coloring can help to play up your features and beef up your beauty confidence. Color analysis requires matching your coloring with a season — the "cool" seasons are winter and summer, and the "warm" seasons are spring and fall.

To find out if you fit into the cool or warm category, grab both a white shirt and a cream-colored shirt from your closet. If you don't have tops in these colors, find a couple of sheets or some pieces of cloth in both white and cream.

Stand in front of a mirror and hold up the white shirt. See how your skin tone looks with the pure white nearest your face. Do you look radiant or washed out?

Now try the test with the cream-colored shirt. Again, check out how your skin, your eyes, and even your hair look next to the off-white choice. Notice a difference? Which color makes you look and feel better?

If pure white complements you best, then you have cool coloring and are either a winter or a summer.

If the cream-colored item looks best on you, then you have warm coloring and are either a spring or a fall.

Now take a look at the chart below and discover which specific season suits you best.

Season Matches

Your hair color	Season
Light golden blond	Spring or Fall
Ash blond (not golden)	Summer or Spring
Strawberry blond/red	Spring or Fall
Light brown	Summer or Spring
Blondish-brown	Summer or Fall
Medium brown	Spring or Fall
Auburn	Fall
Chestnut brown	Spring or Fall

Dark brown	Spring or Winter
Black	Winter

Your eye color

Season

Clear blue, green, or bright hazel	Spring or Fall
Smoky blue or gray	Summer
Hazel, golden brown, or soft turquoise	Spring or Fall
Light hazel or soft blue-green	Summer or Fall
Dark brown or deep hazel	Winter

Your skin tone

Season

Very fair/Never tans	Summer or Spring
Fair or ivory/Burns or freckles easily	Spring, Summer, or Fall
Ivory with pink undertones/Burns in sun then turns to tan	Summer or Spring
Beige, Asian/ Tans fairly easily	Winter
Golden brown, Latina or Black/Tans easily	Winter
Olive or Black/Turns deep bronze in sun	Winter

The seasonal palettes

By now, you should have a good idea of what your color season is. If you're stuck between two seasons, try out colors from both seasons to find out which look best on you and which you prefer. If you stick to selecting colors from your seasonal palette, your own coloring will have a chance to shine!

Here are the colors associated with the different seasons:

Winter

Pure white	Burgundy	Teal blue
Black	Rust	Bright yellow
Charcoal gray	Hot pink	Emerald green
Blood red	Navy	Forest green
Fuchsia	Turquoise	Mint green

Jewelry tone: Silver

Spring

Cream or off-white	Golden brown	Coral
	Camel	Pumpkin
Deep brown	Peach	Golden yellow

Light navy	Aqua	Deep
Yellow-green	Jade green	lavender
Moss green	Teal blue	Violet

Jewelry tone: Gold

Summer

White	Blue-red	Plum
Light gray	Burgundy	Purple
Taupe	Lemon yellow	Periwinkle blue
Khaki	Aqua	Sky blue
Gray-blue	Bright blue	Royal blue
Cocoa brown	Lavender	Navy
Rose		

Jewelry tone: Silver

Fall

Cream or	Salmon	Olive green
soft white	Terra-cotta	Moss green
Pewter gray	Peachy orange	Bronze
Stone	Rust	Copper
Beige	Light navy	Mustard
Golden brown	Eggplant	Deep teal
Dark brown	Golden yellow	Green-blue

Jewelry tone: Gold

Knowing the seasonal color palette that's most flattering to you can make it easier to find the right clothes for you. But remember, your color choices are also a matter of personal preference. Don't *not* buy a gorgeous sweater you love that you think looks great on you just because it's not in one of your seasonal colors. Your colors should serve as a guide. Don't hesitate to try new shades!

Fashions for your figure

Just as everybody is different, every *body* is different, too. A pair of jeans that fits perfectly might end up looking weird on your friend who's the same height and weight as you. How clothes look on you depends on more than just how tall you are and how much you weigh — it has to do with the particular shape of your body. Sound complicated? It's not — you just need a little know-how about what'll look best on your bod. First you need to figure out your body type. Do you have long legs? Short legs? Are you full-sized or so petite you end up searching through little kids' clothes for stuff that'll fit? Find your body type, and then take a look at some of these figure-based fashion secrets.

(But since you are most likely still growing be aware that your body type could change.)

If you are petite, your best bets are:
- dresses and all-one-color outfits
- straight, short skirts in a solid color
- higher-waisted pants and skirts
- short, cropped jackets

If you are large-sized, your best bets are:
- full or A-line skirts
- vertical stripes
- dark-colored clothing
- long jackets

If you are superthin, try:
- layered clothing
- prints and patterns
- flared pants
- horizontal stripes

Your fashion personality

While it's fun to try out all the latest styles, buying clothes just because they are popular can turn up some real duds (no pun intended!). Stick to what suits your personal style preference and you'll wind up buying only those items that are right for you. How do you come to terms with your fashion personality? Figure out which of the statements below could have been said by you:

a. I'm very active and like clothes to be comfortable and low-maintenance.

b. I'm drawn to pretty items, like floral prints or cute dresses.

c. I like to wear clothes that are safe bets — no trying something weird for me!

d. I live to experiment with all the latest and greatest clothes and have no fear of being the first to try a fad.

If you chose *A*, stick to clothing made from natural fabrics like cotton. Be sure to try before you buy — if something is not comfortable on you in the fitting room, it's going to feel even worse once you're wearing it for the whole day. Slim skirts or fitted pants that are too constricting are a definite no for you. You're better off sticking to more relaxed-fitting pants, shorts, and skirts.

If you chose *B*, then you have a feminine, romantic way of dressing. You'll probably be happier with a closetful of skirts and soft-colored fabrics than with bold and dramatic outfits. Pick pastels, prints, and soft and breezy fabrics, like velvet or a silky cotton — nothing stiff for you, thank you very much.

If you chose C, it's best for you to avoid the wild and outrageous trends. While you may love to shop for the newest styles, you'll be much more comfortable if you focus on the classics. Jeans, khakis, turtlenecks, and simple prints can make up the base of your signature style. If you want to try something a little out of the ordinary, start first with accessories.

If you chose D, then probably no trend is too out there for you to try. For you, fashion is about fun and novelty. You'll get bored with your wardrobe if you just stick with the basics. You crave what's new and hip. When it comes to stocking your closet with the essentials, try basics with a twist, like flared jeans or cargo-style khakis. Then accessorize, accessorize, accessorize! The best advice for you: Go for it, girl — give the new looks a whirl.

If you're still a little sketchy on your personal style, ask someone who knows you well for help, like your best friend or your mom. You know how they're often able to look at an outfit in a store and know right away that it's totally *you*? Well, they probably have a good perspective on your personal style and could help you pinpoint it for yourself.

Building a wardrobe from the basics

Putting together a great and stylish wardrobe doesn't have to cost a ton of money. In fact, you probably already have a lot of essential items in your closet. The best way to begin to build your wardrobe is to start with a few basics that never go out of style. Then you can add trendy extras and accessories to develop your own personal look. Your closet basics should include:

Jeans

Some girls can't own enough pairs of jeans, and can you blame them? Jeans are comfortable, fashionable, and affordable. You can dress them up with a cute sweater and a pair of suede loafers, or dress them down with a T-shirt and sneakers. Because you can change their look so easily, you can wear the same pair of jeans more than once during the week and no one will notice! Be sure to have at least one pair that fits well and feels comfortable. From there, the options are endless!

T-shirts

These days, T-shirts are anything but ordinary. While a basic white T is a definite wardrobe essential, you can also fill your drawers with a seemingly endless variety of sizes, styles, and colors. The classic boat-necked T has a round collar and is perfect for wearing alone or under button-down shirts or sweaters. Scoop-necked T's have a rounded, scooped collar and look great on their own and under button-down cardigan sweaters. If a scoop-necked T doesn't suit your style, then go for a slight variation and get a V-necked T instead.

Sneakers

Once found only in the gym or on the playing field, sneakers have risen in the fashion world to become an essential for school and play. Because some sports require special footwear features, such as extra ankle or heel support, it's a good idea to keep your serious sneakers separate from the ones you wear for fashion's sake. Simple canvas sneakers, which are relatively inexpensive, can go with everything from your beloved pair of beat-up jeans to a floral summer dress. If you want to build upon your sneaker wardrobe, experiment with different styles.

Khakis

Khakis have been around for ages, so you can pretty much bet that they aren't going to go out of style anytime soon! So what, exactly, are khakis? Khaki is really a color — kind of a drab olive or tan — that was originally used in the military because of its durability and comfort. It didn't take long for civilians to latch on to these comfy, easy-to-wear, popular pants, though. These days, khakis come in as many shapes and sizes as there are body types — so with a little patience you shouldn't have trouble finding the perfect pair. The best thing about khakis is their color — it goes with just about anything, from denim blue to crimson red and plenty of colors in between.

Sandals

A summer essential! When it's warm out, the last thing you want to do is cram your feet into a pair of covered shoes. A pair of sandals will keep your feet feeling cool — and keep you *looking* pretty cool, too. Sandal styles will change with the seasons, so shop around and find a pair that not only looks cute, but feels comfortable as well.

Sweaters

Regardless of the climate where you live, sweaters can be worn year-round. In the winter, you can wear them under a coat for an extra layer of warmth. In the spring and fall, a sweater with pants or a skirt will keep you comfortable in the cool weather. And during the hot, balmy summer, you can still wear a sweater tied around your shoulders or around your waist — not only can it look great, but it will keep you prepared for cool summer nights or frosty air-conditioned buildings. There are so many types of sweaters out there that you'll want to experiment and try on different styles and colors to find the looks you like the best. Many of the styles below come in short as well as long sleeves. Choose from:

• **turtleneck:** This popular style is one of the best for keeping warm.

• **mock turtleneck:** Essentially, a turtleneck with a shorter neck collar.

• **cardigan:** A round, boat-necked or V-necked sweater that buttons up the front.

- **sweater set:** A cardigan paired with what's called a "shell" — a T-shirt or tank-style sweater worn under the cardigan.
- **V-neck:** The versatile V-neck can be worn over a T-shirt or tied around the shoulders or waist when the weather warms up.
- **boat neck:** A round-collared, pullover sweater.

Sweaters come in a variety of materials, like wool, acrylic, cashmere, and cotton. If your skin itches from wool or angora, stick to a softer material such as cotton or a fabric blend.

Sweater Storage

A good sweater can last a long time, provided you take proper care of it. Unless you want your sweaters to stretch out until they reach your knees, don't hang them on hangers. It's best to keep them folded in drawers or on shelves. As for cleaning sweaters, many can be hand-washed, but follow label instructions and dry-clean if it's recommended. If you do hand-wash sweaters, be sure to lay them flat to dry. If you hang them to dry, they'll stretch and lose their shape.

How to shop like a pro

Clothes shopping shouldn't be a chore; it should be fun! But sometimes staring at endless racks of clothing can leave a girl wishing she were anywhere but crawling the mall. And then there's the pressure of trying to put together an outfit that's both affordable and adorable. Don't fret! Here are a few simple suggestions that will help you be a shopping success.

Going in with ideas

Shopping will be much simpler if you have an idea of what you'd like to purchase before you head to the stores. Take a look through your closet to determine what it is you need or want. Or look through the fashion pages of your favorite magazines or through the wardrobes of your friends for ideas on what to buy. Many magazines feature a "where to shop" guide that can point you in the right direction. Having a clear idea of what you are looking for can save you time and prevent you from buying unwanted stuff.

Is it me?

Be sure to try on clothing before you decide to buy it. Look in the mirror and determine how you feel. Are you uncomfortable in any way? If so, it's not for you! Not quite sure if it's your color? Try looking at it in a different light, say, near a window where there's some natural sunlight. When all else fails, get another opinion.

The ever-important second opinion

Chances are, you go shopping with someone else, like your mom or your best bud. If you're not sure about something, ask her for her opinion. Her perspective may lend a little help when you're stuck on two items or not sure if a style is you. It's always best if your shopping partner knows you well enough to tell you the truth — like when something really doesn't look good on you, even though you may think it's just great. Don't be afraid, though, to trust your own judgment, because in the end you're the one who's going to be wearing what you buy.

Does it fit?

Check to be sure that your clothing choices fit well. Move around a little in them or, if you're buying shoes, walk around the store. Stretch your arms above your head to make sure that tops aren't too tight, and if you have trouble sitting or kneeling in a skirt or pair of pants, forget about 'em! Natural fabrics, such as cotton, may shrink after you wash them. Check the labels to find out if an item's been prewashed, meaning it won't shrink as much, to determine if you should go for a larger size.

The two-day test

Can't decide whether you want to get something? Ask a salesperson to hold it for a day or two. If you still want it the next day, chances are pretty good that it's a keeper. If you've forgotten all about it, don't bother going back to buy it!

I bought it, now I hate it

Even your best shopping efforts can result in mistakes — those clothes that you loved in the store but that make you cringe when you go to wear them for the first time. If you've had a change of heart, don't keep the item and hope it'll grow on you — it won't. But don't worry; most stores allow you to return merchandise for a full refund or exchange it for another item, as long as you have the receipt and the tags are still on the clothing.

Saying adios to unwanted outfits

If your closet is getting full but you never feel like you have enough clothes, it might be time to clear out all those old or unwanted items that are taking up space. But how do you decide which pieces of clothing to part with? Take a look at the list below and apply it to the items in your closet to help decide what gets the heave-ho. Cleaning out your closet also enables you to do a good deed for others — be sure to donate unwanted items that are in good condition to charity.

Get rid of:

- Clothes and shoes you've outgrown
- Items you haven't worn for over a year
- Trendy items you know you won't touch again
- Clothing that's ruined or damaged.

Old clothes, new lives

Having trouble parting with a few fashion finds in your closet . . . even though you've outgrown the items or never wear them anymore? Maybe you don't have to. With a little effort, you can give some of your old clothes a new life. Here are a few fashion makeovers:

Item	Problem	Fix
Jeans	Too short	Cut off the legs and wear them as shorts
Pants or a shirt	Faded colors	Revive or change the colors with dye
T-shirt	Too small	Cut off a sleeve and wear it as a headband
Sweater	Hole in front	Wear as an "accessory," either around your shoulders or tied around your waist
Sandals	Out of style	Use as "shower shoes" when you're camping or at the beach
Sneakers	Trashed	Spare the laces for future shoe emergencies

Accessorizing: Finding just the right finishing touches

Ever notice how some girls seem to have it so together clothes-wise? And even though you may have many of the same kinds of clothes they have, there's just something about the way they put their outfits together that's extra cool? Believe it or not, they may not have a wardrobe that's much bigger or better than yours. It just might be that they know how to add all the right extras to create a finished look that's fabulous.

The key to pulling your look together is in how you accessorize it. Accessories are all the little extras, like jewelry, hats, socks, and even hair stuff like barrettes and headbands. Since many accessories cost less than clothing, you can change your look more easily and more often if you focus on updating your accessories rather than on acquiring a whole new wardrobe. Plus, accessories can be a lot more fun to experiment with than basic clothing items. So don't be shy — give even the wildest accessories a try! You can build your accessory wardrobe by starting with these key pieces.

Jewelry

The one jewelry item that you can wear every day is a watch. You can find watches with metallic gold or silver bands, bands that are bracelet-style, or bands made of plastic, leather, or canvas. It's best to start with a watch that's versatile, one that will go with many or all of your outfits. But versatile doesn't mean boring! Your watch doesn't need to match your outfit perfectly, so if that bright green plastic band keeps calling out your name, go for it! Other items you can add to your jewelry box are necklaces, rings, earrings, and bracelets. A handmade, multicolored friendship bracelet not only looks good but is a nice way to show off your friendship.

Hair accessories

Headbands, barrettes, and ponytail holders are great because they can serve a twofold purpose: make bold fashion statements as well as save you from a bad hair day! It's always a good idea to keep a stash of hair accessories handy. You can wear hair stuff that matches your outfit or go crazy with real out-there styles that can show what a unique individual you are. If your hair is short, opt for cute clips and decorative bobby pins to put a spin on your basic style.

Hats

Just like sneakers, baseball caps have made their way from the courts and playing fields to everyday life. While they're still perfect when you're playing sports or being active, they can also top off your basic jeans–and–T-shirt attire. You don't need to give praise to your favorite teams these days — there are plenty of fashion baseball caps out there to choose from.

Socks

Fancy footwork sometimes requires a little fancy legwork, and a stylish pair of socks can do the trick. There are even shops out there that sell nothing but socks — talk about selection! During winter, your best bet is a pair of tights. Choose solid cotton tights or a pair of ribbed "sweater" tights. Or you could go for some wild patterned or glittery tights for extra impact or on special occasions. When the weather gets a little warmer, put away the tights and put on some ankle socks or kneesocks in colors that match whatever you're wearing.

Spicing up school uniforms

More and more schools, both public and private, are requiring students to wear uniforms. But just because you're stuck wearing a white shirt and a solid-colored skirt or pants doesn't mean you can't add a little flare to your everyday-wear — as long as it's not against school policy. Check out these ABC's for making your uniform unique.

Accessorize: Try out a pair of funky socks or tights and add jewelry, like an array of bracelets or a handmade necklace.

Beef up your backpack: Make your backpack stand out by adding cool pins and key chains or using fabric paint to add your own creative touches. And instead of your basic backpack, why not buy one in a bright color or a funky shape?

Create nail art: Let your nails be your best accessory by applying decals over polish.

Chapter Five

Beauty Confidence

The Key to Loving Your Looks

Now that you've learned a little about enhancing the way you look, it's time to focus on developing your inner beauty. Being confident about who you are and the way you look is just as important, if not more important, than being well groomed and well put together. Being happy with yourself is attractive; people are drawn toward others who have a positive attitude and a healthy outlook. So what if you aren't perfect — no one is — what matters is that you feel great about who you are, imperfections and all. This chapter will help you learn to love your looks and boost your body image.

Overcoming the uglies

Occasionally you may feel a little down on yourself and this is normal. We all have days when we'd just rather bury our heads under the covers and stay put! But when you're overcome with feeling bad about yourself or your looks, it's time for some serious attitude adjustment.

Answer the following questions to find out if you have a negative self-image problem:

• You rarely ever like the image you see in the mirror or what you look like in photos.

• You find it hard to accept compliments about your appearance.

• You often imitate, or even idolize, friends whose looks you admire.

• You say negative things about yourself, either to yourself or to others.

• You feel that your looks are more important than your other characteristics.

• You often feel down or irritable.

• You let your opinions about how you look keep you from doing things, such as joining a sport or going to a party.

• You dread PE because you don't want to be seen in your gym clothes.

If you answered yes to any of the questions above, you could be battling a negative body image. Read on for things you can do to improve the way you feel about yourself.

Don't compare yourself to others: You can look all your life and (even if you have an identical twin) you won't find anyone who looks just like you. That's because, just like snowflakes, each person is unique. It's this uniqueness that makes you beautiful! Don't compare your looks and features to those of a friend, actress, or model. Instead, focus on your own special, positive attributes.

Stop the negative talk: If you're constantly pointing out your every fault and putting yourself down, it'll end up being mighty hard to not believe yourself! Replace those negative remarks you make about yourself with positive ones. And if others make rude remarks about you or are critical, remember that the motivation behind their words is probably anything but honesty. If someone is jealous of you, or feeling bad about herself, she might say mean things about you to make herself feel better. Don't let it get to you!

Get busy: Maybe the reason you worry so much about the way you look or feel is that you spend too much time thinking about it! There are far better things you could be doing than dwelling on your looks. Join a sport or club, or get involved in hobbies and activities you enjoy. If you're bored and start to feel the blues coming on, call a trusted friend for a little pep talk, then move on!

Accentuate the positive: Nobody is blessed with perfection. Even top models have gripes about their physical features. But we all also have a feature or features that we love or are proud of. Maybe it's your cute, perky nose, or your smile that could warm up a room. When you're down on your looks, remind yourself of that feature you love or do something extra to accentuate your positive traits. Also think about those traits that others love in you.

Focus on what's important: OK, so you just got the worst haircut of your life and you feel like retreating to the North Pole until it's grown out. It may seem like the end of the world but, guess what? It's not. Regardless of how it may feel at the moment, you are not judged solely on your hair! There's not a single friend of yours who'd say she likes you just because you have nice hair (and if she did, it's time to go shopping for a new friend!). People are drawn to you for what's inside you, not what's outside. And after the initial reaction to your new do, your buds will barely remember there's anything different about you.

Confidence is a choice: You can wake up in the morning and decide that you feel great and, no matter what hits you that day, you'll keep a positive and happy attitude. Or you can wake up feeling lousy and resign yourself to the fact that you're going to have another bad day. With that kind of negative attitude there's pretty much no way you *won't* have a rotten day. Shift your attitude before it has a chance to ruin your day. When you wake up, no matter how you feel, tell yourself that you look and feel great, and see how much better your day can be!

Conclusion

Beautiful You

You've learned the beauty basics — everything from skin care to hair care to body care. You've discovered how to create a wardrobe that's right for you and you've come to see how important it is to have a positive self-image. These are the tools you'll need to feel good about yourself. While they may seem new to you now, once you begin to incorporate them all into your life, they'll become as routine to you as breathing. Well, maybe they won't come that easily, but you get the idea!

Because you're growing and changing, it's likely your grooming needs and your personal preferences will change, too. What works for you today may fail miserably tomorrow. (C'mon — we all have things in our closet that we look at and wonder, "What was I thinking?!") Be open to exploring and experimenting to find what's right for you. And enjoy the beautiful you!